Sydney Opera House

Sheelagh Matthews
and Heather Kissock

www.av2books.com

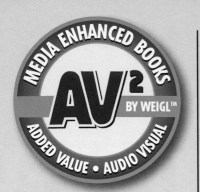

AV² provides enriched content that supplements and complements this book. Weigl's AV² books strive to create inspired learning and engage young minds in a total learning experience.

Your AV² Media Enhanced books come alive with...

Audio
Listen to sections of the book read aloud.

Key Words
Study vocabulary, and complete a matching word activity.

Video
Watch informative video clips.

Quizzes
Test your knowledge.

Embedded Weblinks
Gain additional information for research.

Slide Show
View images and captions, and prepare a presentation.

Try This!
Complete activities and hands-on experiments.

... and much, much more!

Go to **www.av2books.com**, and enter this book's unique code.

BOOK CODE

V 2 1 9 1 6 1

AV² by Weigl brings you media enhanced books that support active learning.

Published by AV² by Weigl
350 5th Avenue, 59th Floor
New York, NY 10118
Websites: www.av2books.com   www.weigl.com

Library of Congress Cataloging-in-Publication Data
Matthews, Sheelagh.
 Sydney Opera House / Sheelagh Matthews and Heather Kissock.
    pages cm. -- (Virtual field trip)
 Includes index.
 ISBN 978-1-4896-2016-3 (hard cover : alk. paper) -- ISBN 978-1-4896-2017-0 (soft cover : alk. paper) --
ISBN 978-1-4896-2018-7 (single use ebook) -- ISBN 978-1-4896-2019-4 (multi use ebook)
 1. Sydney Opera House--Juvenile literature. 2. Utzon, Jrn, 1918-2008--Juvenile literature. 3. Sydney (N.S.W.)--Buildings, structures, etc.--Juvenile literature. I. Kissock, Heather. II. Title.
 NA6840.A79S95 2014
 725'.822099441--dc23
                            2014009345

Printed in the United States of America in North Mankato, Minnesota
1 2 3 4 5 6 7 8 9 0 18 17 16 15 14

052014
WEP310514

Editor: Heather Kissock
Design: Terry Paulhus

Every reasonable effort has been made to trace ownership and to obtain permission to reprint copyright material. The publishers would be pleased to have any errors or omissions brought to their attention so that they may be corrected in subsequent printings.

Weigl acknowledges Getty Images and Alamy as its primary image suppliers for this title.

Contents

What Is the Sydney Opera House?

With its gigantic white sails and its picturesque setting, the Sydney Opera House has captured the imagination of the world. Considered an **architectural** wonder, this structure is a reminder of Australia's coming of age. It was built ahead of its time in terms of style and available technology.

The Sydney Opera House is a world-class performing arts center, a tourist attraction, and a place to hold community events. Its design includes three structures of interlocking, **vaulted** shells. The shells house the building's two main performance venues. The forecourt holds up to 5,000 people for special outdoor concerts and festivals. Smaller performance venues, meeting rooms, restaurants, and shops add to the vibrancy of the complex.

Jutting out into one of the most beautiful natural harbors in the world, the Sydney Opera House greets people from the land, sea, and air. The brilliant-white roof shells of the Sydney Opera House have become an **icon** and a national symbol of Australia.

The roof of the Sydney Opera House was designed to resemble a ship about to set sail, a nod to its harbor location.

Snapshot of Australia

Australia is located in the area known as Oceania. It is both a continent and a country. Australia includes the mainland, the island of Tasmania, and several other smaller islands. New Zealand lies to its southeast, while the Solomon Islands and Vanuatu are found northeast. Indonesia, East Timor, and Papua New Guinea are located north of the continent. Antarctica lies south.

INTRODUCING AUSTRALIA

CAPITAL CITY: Canberra

FLAG:

POPULATION: 23,503,933 (2014 est)

OFFICIAL LANGUAGE: English

CURRENCY: Australian dollar (AUD)

CLIMATE: Temperate in the south and east, and tropical in the north

SUMMER TEMPERATURE: Averages range from 54° to 97° Fahrenheit (12° to 36° Celsius)

WINTER TEMPERATURE: Averages range from 32° to 88° F (0° to 31°C)

TIME ZONES: Australian Eastern Time, Australian Western Time, and Australian Central Standard Time

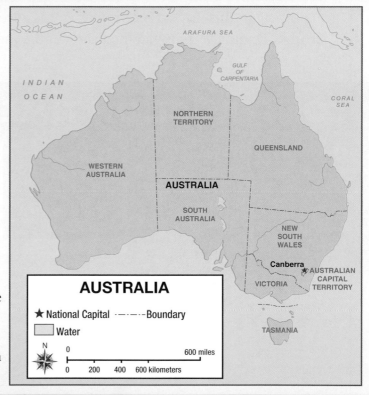

ARAFURA SEA

GULF OF CARPENTARIA

INDIAN OCEAN

CORAL SEA

NORTHERN TERRITORY

QUEENSLAND

WESTERN AUSTRALIA

AUSTRALIA

SOUTH AUSTRALIA

NEW SOUTH WALES

Canberra

VICTORIA

AUSTRALIAN CAPITAL TERRITORY

TASMANIA

AUSTRALIA

★ National Capital —·—·— Boundary

☐ Water

N

0   600 miles

0   200   400   600 kilometers

Australian Symbols

Australia has several official symbols. Some symbols represent the features that distinguish the area from other parts of the world. Others indicate the unique place Australia has in the world.

OFFICIAL FLORAL EMBLEM
Golden Wattle

OFFICIAL GEMSTONE
Opal

A Step Back in Time

The idea for the Sydney Opera House came shortly after World War II. At this time, Australia wanted to become well known around the world for its cultural offerings. In 1956, a competition was announced to design an opera house in Sydney, a major Australian city.

Architects from around the world submitted more than 200 design proposals to compete in this important project. It was a fresh, **innovative** design by Jørn Utzon of Denmark that won the hearts of the judges and the public.

CONSTRUCTION TIMELINE

1952
The government of New South Wales, a state of Australia, decides to build an opera house.

1954
The Opera House Committee is formed. Sydney Harbour is chosen as the site for the structure.

1956
An international design competition is announced.

1957
Danish-born architect Jørn Utzon is declared the winner of the opera house design competition.

1959 to 1973
Construction of the opera house complex takes place.

Tower cranes were brought in from France to lift the roof shells and put them in place.

Construction on Utzon's **tiered**-roof design began in 1959. His concept required the use of new technologies and materials. As a result, construction took much longer and was more expensive than planned. To save costs and time, many of Utzon's plans for the interiors were left out of the structure. On October 20, 1973, the Sydney Opera House opened. Its construction cost $102 million (AUD).

Jørn Utzon left the project when his plans were derailed because of funding problems. Peter Hall, an Australian architect, stepped in to help complete the building.

1973
Queen Elizabeth II declares the Sydney Opera House open on October 20.

1979
The world's largest mechanical pipe organ is installed in the Concert Hall.

1993
An underground parking lot is added to the site.

2004
The Reception Room is renovated to meet Utzon's original design.

2006
A **colonnade** is added to the west side of the building.

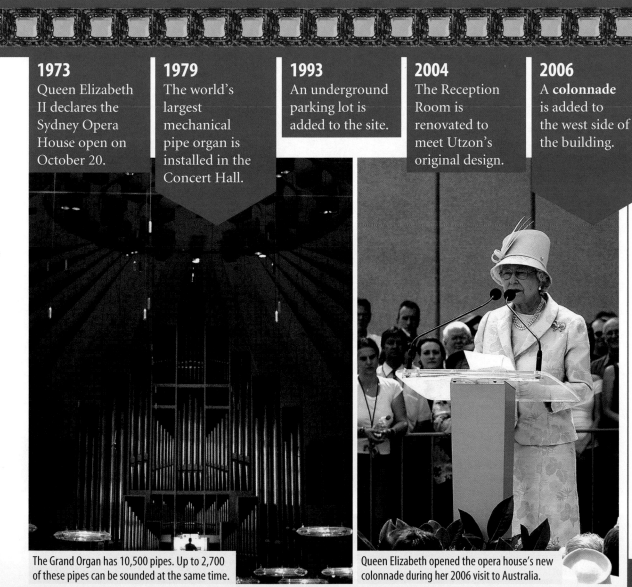

The Grand Organ has 10,500 pipes. Up to 2,700 of these pipes can be sounded at the same time.

Queen Elizabeth opened the opera house's new colonnade during her 2006 visit to Australia.

The Sydney Opera House's Location

The Sydney Opera House is located on a peninsula called Bennelong Point, in Sydney, Australia. Found in the scenic Sydney Harbour, the site is flanked by towering office buildings. It is also near the world's largest steel arch bridge, the Sydney Harbour Bridge. This bridge is known as Sydney's gateway to the Pacific Ocean.

The site was chosen for its picturesque setting and its historical links to the country. The first European settlements were founded near Bennelong Point. The point itself is named after an Aboriginal man who acted as a **liaison** between the British settlers and the Aboriginal community.

The Royal Botanic Gardens are adjacent to the Sydney Opera House.

The Sydney Opera House Today

The Sydney Opera House remains one of the world's best-known performing arts venues. Each year, it hosts almost 3,000 events attended by approximately 2 million people. Another 200,000 visitors take guided tours every year to learn about the history of the building and its behind-the-scenes operations.

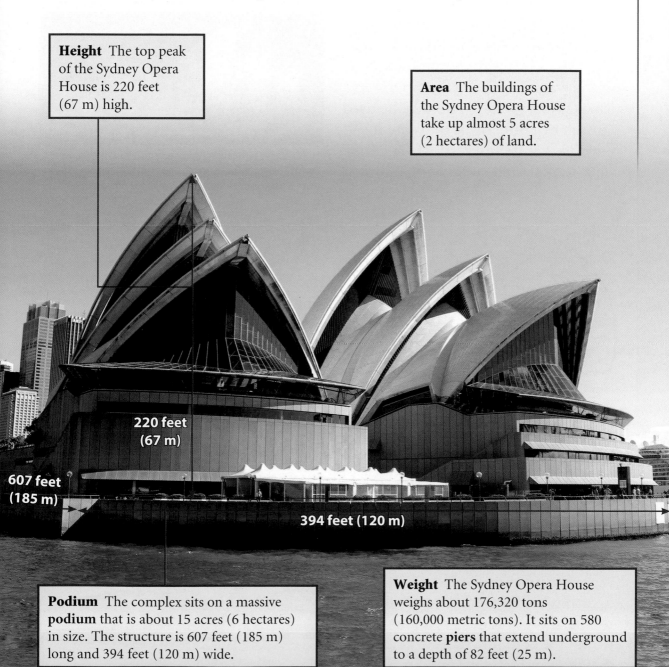

Height The top peak of the Sydney Opera House is 220 feet (67 m) high.

Area The buildings of the Sydney Opera House take up almost 5 acres (2 hectares) of land.

220 feet (67 m)

607 feet (185 m)

394 feet (120 m)

Podium The complex sits on a massive **podium** that is about 15 acres (6 hectares) in size. The structure is 607 feet (185 m) long and 394 feet (120 m) wide.

Weight The Sydney Opera House weighs about 176,320 tons (160,000 metric tons). It sits on 580 concrete **piers** that extend underground to a depth of 82 feet (25 m).

Outside the Sydney Opera House

With its billowing, concrete sails, the Sydney Opera House is an expression of artistic vision. This monumental structure is a feat of innovation and teamwork in engineering, design, and construction.

Roof Shells When drawing up his plans, Utzon wanted to take advantage of the site's beautiful natural setting on the water and its backdrop of urban skyscrapers. To do this, he used natural, **organic** forms to create the reflective vaulted roof shells. The roof shells look like the wedges of an orange and the scales of a fish.

Every year, the Sydney Opera House participates in Vivid Sydney, the city's winter festival. At night, crowds of people visit the harbor to see the building's shells come alive with vibrant patterns and images.

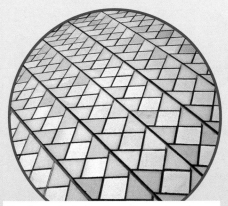
The tiles on the Sydney Opera House are made from clay and crushed stone. They are covered with a transparent glaze to give them their shine.

Tiles The glossy white roof tiles of the Sydney Opera House take on many looks between sunrise and sunset. The tiles were placed on the shells in a **geometrical** pattern, giving them a fishbone look. To contrast the glossy roof areas, **matte** tiles were placed along the shell edges. Without this contrast between the two types of tiles, the roof shells would look like huge, flat surfaces. When light hits the tiles, the contrast gives the building definition, depth, and reflection.

Podium The shells sit on top of the vast, stepped podium, which was inspired by ancient Mayan temples in Mexico. The opera house has more than 1,000 rooms, most of which are found within the podium. Many of these rooms house the building's backstage and technical equipment.

When first built, the Sydney Opera House's podium was the largest concrete form in the southern hemisphere. At its highest point, it is 82 feet (25 m) above sea level.

Broadwalks Extending along two sides of the opera house, the broadwalks serve a variety of functions. They are often used as viewing platforms for events taking place in the harbor. Corporate events and promotions are also staged here. The western broadwalk is sometimes used as a loading area for events taking place in the building.

Seating along the broadwalks encourages people to take some time to appreciate the view Sydney Harbour provides.

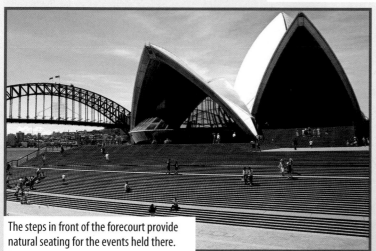

The steps in front of the forecourt provide natural seating for the events held there.

Forecourt The forecourt stretches out in front of the opera house's giant sails and serves as an outdoor performance space. The forecourt is known for its versatility. Besides music concerts, it has hosted art exhibits, television broadcasts, receptions, and other social gatherings.

VIRTUAL TOUR

The Sydney Opera House is open to the public 363 days of the year. It closes only for Christmas and Good Friday.

Inside the Sydney Opera House

The Sydney Opera House was built to showcase the performing arts. Its theaters range from grand concert halls to intimate performance spaces. The number of venues in the building has allowed it to become one of the busiest performing arts centers in the world.

Concert Hall The tallest group of shells house the Concert Hall, the largest of the Sydney Opera House's interior venues. Able to seat 2,679 people, the Concert Hall is home to several of Sydney's key music organizations, including the Sydney Symphony, and has hosted many of the world's top performers. The hall is known for its excellent **acoustics** and high, vaulted ceiling, which gives it a cathedral-like appearance.

The Concert Hall has white birch and brush box paneling. These woods contribute to the quality of the acoustics inside the auditorium.

The Joan Sutherland Theatre was originally known as the Opera Theatre. It was renamed in 2007 to commemorate the singer's contributions to the arts.

Joan Sutherland Theatre
The Joan Sutherland Theatre is named after one of Australia's greatest opera singers. Situated under the center shells, the 1,507-seat theater is the Sydney Opera House's second largest interior venue. The theater plays host to the country's home-grown ballet and opera companies, as well as those from around the world.

Restaurants and Shops The Sydney Opera House provides visitors with a range of dining options. Full-service restaurants allow visitors to sit down to a meal before or after a performance, while buffet-style dining areas provide a more casual atmosphere for people wanting to grab a quick bite. The Sydney Opera House Shop is located on the lower concourse of the building. Here, visitors can buy unique gifts and souvenirs.

Some of the opera house's restaurants offer outside dining as well.

The Sydney Opera House recording studio cost approximately $4.3 million (AUD) to set up. It began operating in 2004.

Recording Studio In the podium underneath the main sails lies the Sydney Opera House's recording studio. The studio contains state-of-the-art technology needed to record musical performances, stage plays, and movies. It is linked to all of the interior venues, so performances can be recorded as they are taking place. These performances can be recorded for future release or for live broadcasts.

Playhouse With only 398 seats, the Playhouse is one of the Sydney Opera House's smaller theaters. It was originally intended for small-scale music recitals. However, it is now also used to stage plays, movies, presentations, and conferences. Several of Sydney's arts organizations use the Playhouse for their productions, taking advantage of the small, intimate setting.

The Playhouse is best suited to shows that focus on the performers. It does not have space for large sets or constant scene changes.

Big Ideas behind the Sydney Opera House

The construction of the Sydney Opera House was a rare and outstanding architectural achievement. Building it required special construction methods and materials. Many engineers, building contractors, architects, and manufacturers had to work together.

In all, 2,194 precast concrete roof sections were used on the Sydney Opera House.

Spherical Geometry

Utzon's inspiration for the opera house's shells was an orange that had been cut up into pieces. He used the pieces to see how the roof shells should be put together. Utzon used a sphere as a model for the roof shells. He gave each shell the same amount of **curvature**. This meant all of the shell exteriors would have a clearly defined geometry in common. In fact, if all of the pieces of the roof of the Sydney Opera House were put together, they would form a sphere. This use of spherical geometry made it possible for the shell components to be **prefabricated** and mass produced.

The Properties of Glass

With 67,005 square feet (6,225 square m) of glass in the structure, the **properties** of glass had to be accounted for when the Sydney Opera House was designed. Solar energy can readily pass through glass, raising the temperature inside the enclosure. Glass also conducts sound, which can be a problem in a noisy harbor. To deal with potential heat and sound transfer problems, a special type of glass was made. Two layers of this glass stop the sound of ships from affecting performances in the halls. These layers also help **insulate** the structure from the heat of the Sun's rays.

The Sydney Opera House's glass walls were inspired by waterfalls. Their diagonal slant is meant to reflect the motion of falling water.

Science at Work at the Sydney Opera House

Heavy lifting is a large part of building construction. Sydney Opera House workers relied on cranes to raise and install heavy concrete roof sections. To prepare the site for construction, more than 39,238 cubic yards (30,000 cubic m) of rock and rubble had to be removed from Sydney Harbour. This feat was done using mechanical shovels.

Some cranes use movable pulleys. This type of pulley allows an object to be transported horizontally.

Pulleys

A pulley is a freely turning wheel with a grooved rim over which a belt or chain is guided. Pulleys help raise and lower heavy loads by changing the direction of a pulling force. Mechanical shovels use pulleys to do their job. In this case, a vehicle with a large bucket on a mechanical arm has a series of power-driven steel cables that run through pulleys to raise and lower the bucket. Cranes, machines that lift and move heavy construction materials and equipment into place, use pulleys to operate. Both pieces of machinery played large roles in building the Sydney Opera House.

Hydraulics

A hydraulic system has two pistons in cylinders filled with an **incompressible** liquid, often oil. The oil is pumped to the cylinders and pistons through valves. The pistons are connected by a pipe. When pressure is applied to one piston, the force is transferred to the second piston through the oil. As one piston is pushed down, the other is lifted by the oil. This back-and-forth movement powers the machine. Hydraulic shovels use two pistons—one at the elbow of the shovel's arm and another to turn the bucket. These pistons work with motors to operate the digging and rotating motion of the shovel.

Hydraulic shovels can remove more than 35 cubic feet (1 cubic m) of dirt at a time.

VIRTUAL TOUR

The Sydney Opera House has 1,056,000 ceramic roof tiles covering its shells. The tiles were made in Sweden.

The Sydney Opera House's Builders

Architects, engineers, carpenters, concrete workers, plumbers, electricians, stonemasons, crane operators, general laborers, and many others played an important role in the construction of the Sydney Opera House. Many of the design elements in this structure had never been attempted before. Those involved in building the Sydney Opera House used their knowledge, skills, and experience to find innovative solutions to construction challenges.

Utzon came from a family of sailors. He used his maritime background to design the Sydney Opera House.

Jørn Utzon Architect

The architect who designed the Sydney Opera House was a young man hailing from halfway around the world. Born in Copenhagen, Denmark, Jørn Utzon learned how to sculpt in high school and decided to become an artist. He began studying at Copenhagen's Royal Academy of Arts in 1937. Soon, he discovered he had a talent for designing structures. In 1942, he graduated with a gold medal for architecture. This was the first of many awards he received for his work. Following his studies, Utzon spent the next 10 years traveling and working in many parts of the world, including Europe, Australia, Japan, India, Mexico, and the United States.

In 1956, Utzon began working on his entry for the Sydney Opera House design competition. After being announced the winner, he worked on the project in Denmark until 1963, making visits each year to Sydney. In early 1963, Utzon moved to Sydney to continue his work on the project. However, due to problems with construction delays and cost overruns, Utzon left the project in 1966.

Still, Utzon's career as an architect continued to blossom. He was hired to design more buildings, including the Kuwait National Assembly Complex and the Bagsvaerd Church. In 2003, Jørn Utzon won the Pritzker Architecture Prize. Winning this award is the one of the highest honors an architect can receive. He died five years later at the age of 90.

Bagsvaerd Church is one of the few buildings Utzon designed for his homeland. Located in the Danish town of Bagsvaerd, the church is known for its curved, cloud-like ceilings.

Structural engineers often visit the construction site to confer with other members of the building team.

Structural Engineers

Structural engineers often work with architects, other engineers, and construction contractors. They help design load-bearing structures, such as roofs, bridges, towers, and buildings. Structural engineers carry out inspections at different stages of the building process to make sure the structure can withstand different forces, such as wind, rain, and vibration. They make sure structures are built safe, strong, and stable.

Concrete Finishers

Construction workers that specialize in concrete are called concrete finishers. They work both indoors and out, depending on the task. Concrete finishers pour wet concrete into casts, or molds, and spread it to a desired thickness. They level and smooth the surface and edges of the concrete. To give the concrete different effects, they apply various finishes to the surface. These finishes give the concrete a smooth or patterned appearance. Concrete finishers also repair, waterproof, and restore concrete surfaces. This physical work involves lifting heavy bags of cement, bending, and kneeling.

Concrete finishers must know how to age concrete perfectly in order for it to have maximum strength.

Landscape Architects

The goal of a landscape architect is to create harmony between architectural structures and the site on which they are located. Landscape architects create, manage, and preserve environments so that they are both useful and visually appealing. They plan parks and help design green spaces to fit a building's design and use. To do this, they study the landscape of sites, including slope, plants, soil, and how water drains. Their landscape designs take into account social, economic, environmental, and artistic factors.

Landscape architects can work on projects ranging from designing residential yards to repurposing former industrial sites.

Similar Structures around the World

Many different buildings have captured the attention of the world. Part of their appeal is the amount of effort and time involved in their construction. Mainly, however, it is the building's appearance that draws people to it. Innovation in design and the effective use of materials have made certain buildings stand out throughout time in all parts of the world.

Parthenon

BUILT: 443 BC
LOCATION: Athens, Greece
DESIGN: Ictinus and Kallicrates
DESCRIPTION: The Parthenon is one of the best-known buildings on the **Acropolis** in Athens. With its mighty columns, the Parthenon is referred to as "the most perfect structure of **antiquity**." In ancient times, the Parthenon's purpose was to house the treasury of Athens, similar to modern-day banks.

Neuschwanstein Castle is one of the most visited castles in Europe. Every year, approximately 1.4 million people tour the castle's rooms and grounds.

Besides housing the treasury, the Parthenon was also a temple. It was built to honor the goddess Athena.

Neuschwanstein Castle

BUILT: 1892
LOCATION: Bavaria, Germany
DESIGN: Christian Yank, Eduard von Riedel, Georg Dollman, Julius Hofmann
DESCRIPTION: This castle was built by Bavaria's King Ludwig II. It was modern for the time, as it included a central heating system and hot and cold running water. Walt Disney used this structure as the model for the castles in his theme parks.

Solomon R. Guggenheim Museum

BUILT: 1959
LOCATION: New York City, United States
DESIGN: Frank Lloyd Wright
DESCRIPTION: This round-shaped building takes on a circle shape inside as well. It features oval-shaped columns and a huge concrete spiral walkway. To view the art inside, visitors start at the top of the walkway and work their way down.

The Solomon R. Guggenheim Museum is known around the world for its large collection of modern art.

Taj Mahal

BUILT: 1653 AD
LOCATION: Agra, India
DESIGN: Mohammed Isa Afandi, Ustad Ahmed Lahori
DESCRIPTION: It took 20,000 laborers and the skill of many artists to build the Taj Mahal. This jewel-embedded **mausoleum** is known as a monument to eternal love. Shah Jahan built the Taj Mahal to contain the remains of his wife, Mumtaz Mahal.

The Taj Mahal is made of marble. It is decorated with up to 28 different types of precious and semi-precious stones.

Issues Facing the Sydney Opera House

The Sydney Opera House is the highlight of Sydney Harbour. However, its location works against the building in a number of ways. Some of the problems it faces stem from environmental factors. Others are a result of being in a growing city.

WHAT IS THE ISSUE?

Urban development is encroaching on the area around the Sydney Opera House.

The ebb and flow movement of the ocean puts pressure on the building's foundation.

EFFECTS

Open space around the Sydney Opera House is important to preserve views to and from the building. If new buildings are constructed too close to the opera house, these views may be obstructed.

Cracks and chips appear that can become dangerous to the stability of the structure.

ACTION TAKEN

In 2005, the Sydney Opera House was named a national landmark. It was given protected status when it was added to Australia's National Heritage List. It later became a **UNESCO World Heritage Site**. Laws were put in place to ensure that the Sydney Opera House would not be harmed by future development.

The Australian government began developing a conservation plan for the Sydney Opera House in 1993. In 2002, it set aside more than $69 million (AUD) for long-term care of the structure. Some of this money is invested in protecting the structure's foundation.

Exploring Spherical Geometry

Flat, or plane, geometry is the most common type of geometry. It deals with lines and triangles on flat surfaces. However, many types of surfaces are not flat. Some surfaces are curved like spheres. To measure a sphere, mapmakers, architects, and engineers use a type of geometry called spherical geometry.

Spherical geometry has some interesting differences from plane geometry. For example, in plane geometry, the angles within a triangle always add up to 180 degrees. In contrast, triangles on a curved or spherical surface can be greater than 180 degrees. Try this activity to see how different it can be to work in a spherical environment.

Instructions

1. Stand up. Let your arms hang down loosely beside your body.

2. Make a fist with your right hand. Leave your thumb sticking straight out. Your thumb should be pointing forward.

3. Keep your right arm straight, and do not twist your right wrist for the rest of the exercise.

4. Swing your right arm up and out to the side. Notice the circular arc you made with your arm. Your thumb should still be pointing forward. Do not let your arm drop.

5. Next, swing your right arm forward, so that it points straight ahead. Notice the circular arc that you made with your arm, and the new direction that your thumb is pointing. Your thumb should now be pointing left.

6. Next, swing your right arm down so that it rests at your side. Notice the circular arc you made with your arm. Your thumb will be pointing to the left. Your right arm has returned to its starting position, but your thumb is now twisted by 90 degrees. In this activity, your hand is a point moving around a sphere.

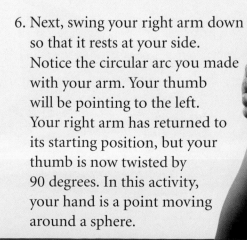

Sydney Opera House Quiz

Q Where is the Sydney Opera House located?

A The Sydney Opera House is located in Bennelong Point, Sydney Harbour, Sydney, Australia.

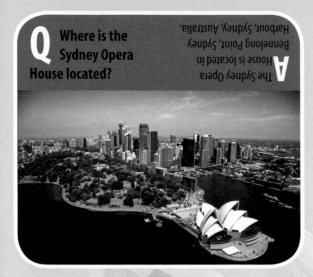

Q Who designed the Sydney Opera House?

A Jørn Utzon designed the Sydney Opera House.

Q How many years did it take to build the Sydney Opera House?

A It took 14 years to build the Sydney Opera House.

Q What type of base is used for the Sydney Opera House?

A The Sydney Opera House was built on a platform, or "podium," an architectural concept used in the construction of Mayan pyramid temples.

Key Words

acoustics: the features of an area, or of things inside that area, that dictate how sound is heard

acropolis: the fortified part of a Greek city

antiquity: of ancient times

architectural: based on the design of buildings

colonnade: a row of columns supporting a roof

curvature: being curved or bent and the degree of that curve

geometrical: based on a type of mathematics that studies shapes and objects and how angles, points, lines, planes, and solids relate

icon: a symbol of great importance

incompressible: not reduced in volume by increased pressure

innovative: featuring new and original methods and ideas

insulate: to prevent heat or sound from passing through easily

liaison: a person who helps groups work together

matte: a dull, lusterless finish

mausoleum: a large, detailed structure that houses a tomb

organic: of or derived of living matter

piers: solid supports designed to sustain vertical pressure

podium: a low wall forming a base for a construction

prefabricated: produced something in a standardized way, such as sections of a building, to make something before it is needed on the job site

properties: qualities or attributes

tiered: arranged in layers

UNESCO World Heritage Site: a site designated by the United Nations to be of great cultural worth to the world and in need of protection

vaulted: arched

Index

Log on to www.av2books.com

AV² by Weigl brings you media enhanced books that support active learning. Go to www.av2books.com, and enter the special code found on page 2 of this book. You will gain access to enriched and enhanced content that supplements and complements this book. Content includes video, audio, weblinks, quizzes, a slide show, and activities.

AV² Online Navigation

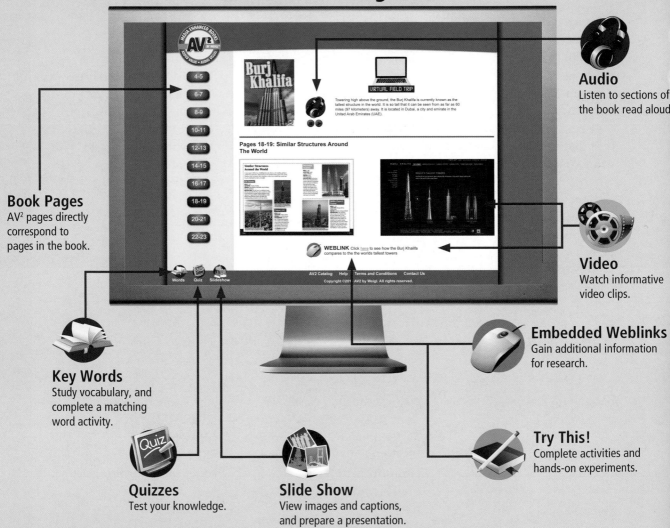

Book Pages
AV² pages directly correspond to pages in the book.

Audio
Listen to sections of the book read aloud

Video
Watch informative video clips.

Embedded Weblinks
Gain additional information for research.

Key Words
Study vocabulary, and complete a matching word activity.

Quizzes
Test your knowledge.

Slide Show
View images and captions, and prepare a presentation.

Try This!
Complete activities and hands-on experiments.

AV² was built to bridge the gap between print and digital. We encourage you to tell us what you like and what you want to see in the future.

Sign up to be an AV² Ambassador at www.av2books.com/ambassador.